My First Acrostic
All About Me

Lancashire

Edited By Machaela Gavaghan

First published in Great Britain in 2019 by:

Young Writers
Remus House
Coltsfoot Drive
Peterborough
PE2 9BF
Telephone: 01733 890066
Website: www.youngwriters.co.uk

All Rights Reserved
Book Design by Ashley Janson
© Copyright Contributors 2019
Softback ISBN 978-1-83928-587-5

Printed and bound in the UK by BookPrintingUK
Website: www.bookprintinguk.com
YB0426T

Dear Reader,

Dear Reader,

Welcome to a fun-filled book of acrostic poems!

Here at Young Writers, we are delighted to introduce our new poetry competition for KS1 pupils, *My First Acrostic: All About Me*. Acrostic poems are an enjoyable way to introduce pupils to the world of poetry and allow the young writer to open their imagination to a range of topics of their choice. The colourful and engaging entry forms allowed even the youngest (or most reluctant) of pupils to create a poem using the acrostic technique, and with that, encouraged them to include other literary techniques such as similes and description. Here at Young Writers we are passionate about introducing the love and art of creative writing to the next generation and we love being a part of their journey.

From pets to family, from hobbies to idols, these pupils have shaped and crafted their ideas brilliantly, showcasing their budding creativity. So, we invite you to proceed through these pages and take a glimpse into these blossoming young writers' minds. We hope you will relish these poems as much as we have.

Contents

Blackshaw Primary School, Bolton

Ashleigh Martin (5)	1
Annabelle York (6)	2
Harrison Taylor (5)	3
Colby-Jak Gears-Brooks (6)	4
Brandon Greenhalgh (5)	5
Olivia Moscrop (5)	6
Thomas Benali (5)	7
Amelia Ashton (5)	8
Nathan Zachary Barlow (5)	9
Emily Hilton (5)	10
Jacob James McGregor (5)	11
Molly Moreton (5)	12
Laila-Marie Makin (5)	13
Poppy Prescott (5)	14
Lola Grace Gears-Spence (5)	15

Brookhouse Primary School, Blackburn

Dania Moosa (6)	16
Eshaal Farrukh (6)	17
Isra Pathan (6)	18
Zoyah Fiaz (7)	19
Ahmed Hussain (6)	20
Raheem Hussain (6)	21
Tayyabah Patel (6)	22
Mohammad Patel (6)	23
Aaminah Javed Gamgori (6)	24
Ummekulsum Javed Gamgori (6)	25
Sarah Deen (6)	26
Tawheed Hussain (6)	27
Maira Soomro (6)	28
Mohammed Ayaan Saghir (6)	29
Ridah Kayani (6)	30
Abu Bakr Mahmood (6)	31

Ightenhill Primary School, Burnley

Dale Hoyle (7)	32
Tommie Hartley (7)	33
Bobby Jack Watkiss (6)	34
Paris Golden (6)	35
Oscar Kelly (6)	36
Tyler Mitchell (6)	37
Oakley Howorth (7)	38
Kody Ashworth (7)	39
Felicity Gardner (6)	40
Archie Huggon (6)	41
Jack Habiak (5)	42
Braeden Lee David Robinson (6)	43
Charlie Bannister (6)	44
Essika Bennett (6)	45
Kian Fitzpatrick (6)	46
Lucy Skaife (6)	47
Jake Knight (7)	48
Emily Bradshaw (6)	49
Amaya Trapanese (6)	50
Daisie Dakota Skyla Humber (6)	51
Olivia Steer (6)	52
Star Krasowski (6)	53
Gracy Mai Dean (6)	54
Mason Hitchon (6) & Chloe	55
Ruby Faragher (7)	56

Intack Primary School, Blackburn

Abu Hurairah (6)	57
Mohammad Ch (6)	58
Fatimah Zahra S (6)	59

Kornelia Zietek (6)	60
Zack Evans (6)	61
Mariam Malik (6)	62
Jayjay Koselka (6)	63
Jessica Archer (6)	64
Arianna Patel (6)	65
Michael John D'Alessandro (7)	66
Scarlet Maxwell (6)	67
Arissa Akhtar (6)	68
Declan H (6)	69
Macey Jade Harrison (7)	70
Lawson Yates (6)	71
Salman Mahmad (6)	72
Ayesha Malic (6)	73
Marva Sheid (7)	74
Malcom Davies (6)	75
Marija Kiurt (6)	76
Alicia Wright (6)	77
Tillie S (6)	78
Eduard Kevorkyan (6)	79
Eesaa Foolat (6)	80
Eshal Rhman (6)	81
Alfie Donnelly (6)	82
Moosa Nasir (6)	83
Adrian Babiarz (6)	84
Harry Andrew Hodgeon (6)	85
Gwen Mellor-Best (6)	86
Ella Maxwel (6)	87
Salahuddin Awan Ahmed (6)	88
Wasiq Nasar (6)	89
Eamon Escels (7)	90
Lawy Hassan (7)	91
Skye Amber Louise Robinson (7)	92
Lily Hargreaves (6)	93
Lexi Mc (6)	94
Musa Solkar (6)	95
Leon Malankowski (6)	96

Springfield Community Primary School, Burnley

Nina Sadowska (6)	97
Ibrahim Ali (6)	98
Isaac Stanworth	99
Layla-Mae Pounder (6)	100
Holly-Mae Creelman (6)	101
Ibrahim Tariq (6)	102
Maisie Dean (6)	103
Christopher Neil Macdonald (6)	104
Aeryn Halson (6)	105
Irfa Amir (6)	106
Olivia-Rose Debra Ellis (6)	107
Noah Franklin (6)	108
Thomas Callum Fuller (6)	109
Amy Walker (6)	110
Coby Ewens (6)	111

St Luke & St Philip's CE Primary School, Blackburn

Saalih Kamran (6)	112
Mohammad Ismail (6)	113
Mark Madden (6)	114
Ella Dean (6)	115
Alicja Karwowska (6)	116
Rahaan Craigh (6)	117
Amanda-Jayne Bleeks (6)	118
Hope McCleary (6)	119
Lexi Freya Mcalinden (6)	120
Samme Abdullah (6)	121
Daniel Obiefna (6)	122
Daniyal Tanveer (6)	123
Mikolaj Sobiecki	124
Jordan Morrison (6)	125
Bradley Greenwood (6)	126
Rhiana Mercer (6)	127
Awab Haroon (6)	128
Raul Cosmin (6)	129

St Patrick's RC Primary School, Walton-le-Dale

Florence Rowen (6)	130
Eva Mackenzie (6)	131
Caitlin Parker (6)	132
Scarlet-Rose Mayne (6)	133
Brodie Pilkington (7)	134
Amelia Jewes-Bonage (6)	135
Brooke Amelia Furesz (6)	136
Oliver James Johnstone (6)	137
Seamus Alty (6)	138
Kaleb Colapinto (6)	139
Hollie Calvert (6)	140
Alfie Parkinson (7)	141
Jacob Walmsley (6)	142
Connor Boyle (6)	143
Maisie Wright (6)	144
Emily Gudgeon (6)	145
Jessica Leighton (6)	146
Archie Joseph Lord (6)	147
Alfie Sean Hodson (6)	148
Evan Beau Turner (7)	149
Erin Boyle (6)	150

St Paul's CE Primary School, Astley Bridge

Muhammad Mogra (6)	151
Laila Khan (6)	152
Sobaan Raza (6)	153
Zaid R'Honi (6)	154
Abdoulie Bah (6)	155
Zainab Mitha (7)	156
Muhammad Yasin (6)	157
Reyhand Ali (6)	158
Zakariya Maka (7)	159
Maryam Buksh (6)	160
Buella Koteh (7)	161
Hayaa Zaidi (6)	162
Aaminah Patel (6)	163
Mariam Doodhwala (6)	164
Hidayah Chhadat (6)	165
Chidinma Nwandiogo (6)	166
Katie-Lee Dawson (6)	167
Rahman Ahmed (6)	168
Faria Dakri (6)	169
Abdullahi Muhidin Ali (6)	170
Faraj Sasi (6)	171
Faraz Ahmad (7)	172
Aaryan Nazir (6)	173
Aymen (7)	174
Neema Hekeleme (6)	175
Bella Farrell (6)	176
Maha Aslam (6)	177
Jack Buckthorpe	178

St Pius X Catholic Preparatory School, Fulwood

Husna Bux (7)	179
Zaid Khan (7)	180

The Poems

My Poem

A pples, nice and juicy
S ausages are meaty
H orrid Henry likes to play
L .O.L. dolls are made from plastic
E lephants have trunks
I ce cream is cold
G rass grows and it is green
H aribos are chewy.

Ashleigh Martin (5)
Blackshaw Primary School, Bolton

My Poem

A pples are crunchy
N ana is the best
N aps are fun
A nn is a singer
B ella is my best friend
E llie is my best cousin
L emons are sour
L emonade is fizzy
E lephants are fast.

Annabelle York (6)
Blackshaw Primary School, Bolton

My Poem

H aribos are yummy
A pples are tangy
R ivers are fast
R abbits are fluffy
I ce cream that is bubblegum
S nakes are slimy
O ranges are juicy
N ew toys from the shop.

Harrison Taylor (5)
Blackshaw Primary School, Bolton

My Poem

C omputers are fun
O ranges are sour
L emons are sweet
B aths are hot
Y o-yos are fun

J okes are funny
A pples are sweet
K angaroos are fun.

Colby-Jak Gears-Brooks (6)
Blackshaw Primary School, Bolton

My Poem

B irds like to sing
R ats are cheeky
A pples are green
N uggets can be golden
D ogs bark very loud
O ranges are the best
N ice hot baths are good.

Brandon Greenhalgh (5)
Blackshaw Primary School, Bolton

My Poem

O ctopuses have eight legs
L emonade that is fizzy
I ce cream that tastes nice
V anilla ice cream is the best
I like L.O.L. dolls
A crostics are fun.

Olivia Moscrop (5)
Blackshaw Primary School, Bolton

My Poem

T arantulas are scary
H ot baths are good
O ctopuses have eight legs
M onster Munch are good
A pples are sweet
S nakes are wiggly.

Thomas Benali (5)
Blackshaw Primary School, Bolton

My Poem

A pples are sweet
M ummy is the best
E lephants are big
L ollies are yummy
I ce cream is cold
A nnabelle is my best friend.

Amelia Ashton (5)
Blackshaw Primary School, Bolton

My Poem

N ice hot baths
A pples are juicy
T omatoes are red
H ot dogs are tasty
A pples are sweet
N ightmares are scary.

Nathan Zachary Barlow (5)
Blackshaw Primary School, Bolton

My Poem

E ggs and chips for tea
M ice that run around
I ce pops that are yummy
L .O.L. dolls are fun
Y oghurt tastes sweet.

Emily Hilton (5)
Blackshaw Primary School, Bolton

My Poem

J uice is sweet and juicy
A pples are crunchy
C ats are great climbers
O ranges make juice
B ikes are fast.

Jacob James McGregor (5)
Blackshaw Primary School, Bolton

My Poem

M ondays are the best
O range juice is yummy
L aughing at jokes
L emonade is sweet
Y o-yos are round.

Molly Moreton (5)
Blackshaw Primary School, Bolton

My Poem

L ollipops are lovely
A pples are crunchy
I ce cream is icy
L ights are bright
A lligators bite you!

Laila-Marie Makin (5)
Blackshaw Primary School, Bolton

My Poem

P ugs are the best
O ranges are sweet
P urple is the best
P uppies are very cute
Y oghurt is yummy.

Poppy Prescott (5)
Blackshaw Primary School, Bolton

My Poem

L emonade is yummy
O ranges are nice fruits
L .O.L. dolls are fun to play with
A lligators are scary!

Lola Grace Gears-Spence (5)
Blackshaw Primary School, Bolton

Dania

U nbelievably, this is the cutest thing I've ever seen
N othing is cuter than this animal
I love feeding this cute animal with grass
C ute animals are the best
O ut on a sunny day is lovely
R ainbow wings look lovely on cute animals
N ice is a kind thing that an animal does.

Dania Moosa (6)
Brookhouse Primary School, Blackburn

Unicorn

U nbelievably, the cutest animal in the world
N othing as cute as this creature
I maginative animal
C uddly creatures are my favourite animals
O ver the hills and far off it goes
R unning as fast as it can
N ever ever see them again.

Eshaal Farrukh (6)
Brookhouse Primary School, Blackburn

Morocco

M cDonald's is where I eat
O ctopus statue
R oads were bumpy
O n the beach, I was collecting seashells and rocks
C lothes for hot places
C lothes were fancy in the shops
O n the plane, I ate crips.

Isra Pathan (6)
Brookhouse Primary School, Blackburn

Unicorns

U nbelievably adorable
N othing is cuter as them
I maginative creature
C orns and ice cream are their food
O riginal things
R ings and necklaces are their favourites
N ice things are the best for them.

Zoyah Fiaz (7)
Brookhouse Primary School, Blackburn

Pakistan

P arty at the fair
A lways ride on bikes
K icking a ball with my cousins
I had an ice cream
S wings
T he toy shops
A lways swimming in the morning
N othing better than this country.

Ahmed Hussain (6)
Brookhouse Primary School, Blackburn

Morocco

M cDonald's is what I ate
O n the plane I had chocolate
R oads are bumpy
O n holiday I was in a nice hotel
C ars everywhere
C ool at the pool
O n the holiday I was in a van.

Raheem Hussain (6)
Brookhouse Primary School, Blackburn

Tayyabah

T errific, amazing girl
A mazing girl
Y esterday I went to the park
Y oghurt is my favourite food
A mazing girl
B ees are the best animal
A mazing music
H appy girl.

Tayyabah Patel (6)
Brookhouse Primary School, Blackburn

Unicorn

U nbelievably cute
N othing as cute as this
I t's my favourite
C ars are my favourite vehicles
O ranges are my fruit
R unning as fast as I can
N ever ever back again.

Mohammad Patel (6)
Brookhouse Primary School, Blackburn

Aaminah

A mazing learner
A lways imagines playing music
M um and Dad are the best
I ce cream lover
N uts are my favourite
A ctimel is my favourite
H appy friends forever.

Aaminah Javed Gamgori (6)
Brookhouse Primary School, Blackburn

Unicorn

U nstoppable
N othing as cute
I ce cream is their favourite food
C utest animal ever
O utstanding animals
R ainbow-coloured animal
N ice animals in the world.

Ummekulsum Javed Gamgori (6)
Brookhouse Primary School, Blackburn

Sarah

S weets are my favourite
A lways playing with my sister on the trampoline
R abbits are my favourite animal
A ways going to the Mosque
H ot chocolate is my favourite drink.

Sarah Deen (6)
Brookhouse Primary School, Blackburn

Unicorn

U nbelievable animal
N ice colour
I ce cream is their favourite food
C one sitting on their head
O riginal looks
R ainbow coloured
N othing magical.

Tawheed Hussain (6)
Brookhouse Primary School, Blackburn

Maira

M agical girl with shiny shoes
A mazing runner with a glittery bag
I maginary power girl
R ainbow power that has rainbow hair
A stonishing girl that has fire power.

Maira Soomro (6)
Brookhouse Primary School, Blackburn

School

S haring is caring
C aring is what we do
H onesty is in our policy
O ur writing is the best
O utside we play football
L earning at school is fun.

Mohammed Ayaan Saghir (6)
Brookhouse Primary School, Blackburn

Ridah

R unning girl
I ce cream lover
D rums make lots of noise
A mazing girl
H appy friends forever.

Ridah Kayani (6)
Brookhouse Primary School, Blackburn

Mouse

M y pet
O ur mouse sniffs cheese
U nder the table, it scurries
S ure is fast
E ats its cheese.

Abu Bakr Mahmood (6)
Brookhouse Primary School, Blackburn

Dale

M y teachers always teach us.
R eally good teachers mean good schools.
S chool is good, everything is good. I love my life.

W ill I go home?
I don't attack, I hug people.
L ike people, I am kind and good,
K ind and helpful.
I nteresting lessons.
N ever cross.
S miles a lot.
O n top of the world.
N ever late.

Dale Hoyle (7)
Ightenhill Primary School, Burnley

Class Five

C lass Five is the best.
L ooking in the books.
A wonderful place to be.
S miles all around.
S eeing from the window of my car.

F ive is the best.
I s Five a good class?
V ery hard-working.
E veryone is friendly.

Tommie Hartley (7)
Ightenhill Primary School, Burnley

Football

F ootie is my favourite thing
O ranges are good for you
O n the field you can play football
T alk to the referee
B all
A pples are good for you
L isten to the referee
L ast drink, footballers!

Bobby Jack Watkiss (6)
Ightenhill Primary School, Burnley

Football

F ootball is the best.
O h, I am good at football.
O h, I like to play football.
T errific at football.
B ack of the net.
A lways fun.
L ove football.
L earning to play football.

Paris Golden (6)
Ightenhill Primary School, Burnley

Football

F ootball is a game.
O kay, pass to my friends.
O kay, good goal.
T ry to score some goals.
B ut football is the best game.
A ttack.
L ike it.
L ike it!

Oscar Kelly (6)
Ightenhill Primary School, Burnley

Animals

A nimals all have four legs
N ot got stripes
I t has a green eye
M agic animals
A nimals all like food
L icking their lips
S niffing me, they make friends.

Tyler Mitchell (6)
Ightenhill Primary School, Burnley

Football

F antastic game.
O ut of this world.
O lympic Games.
T errific fun.
B alls go over the line.
A lways fun.
L eague.
L ife is good with football.

Oakley Howorth (7)
Ightenhill Primary School, Burnley

Science

S cience is the best.
C ool science.
I s science cool to you?
E xciting science.
N ice science.
C ool and mad experience.
E xperimenting in science today.

Kody Ashworth (7)
Ightenhill Primary School, Burnley

Cheese

C heese is sweet
H ard or soft
E very day of the week I have some
E ating cheese makes me happy
S tringy cheese is the best
E very day I think of cheese.

Felicity Gardner (6)
Ightenhill Primary School, Burnley

Football

F antastic football
O ver the net
O lympic games
T errific fun
B e a good footballer
A lways fall
L ove it
L ook at the game.

Archie Huggon (6)
Ightenhill Primary School, Burnley

Football

F antastic game
O ver the net
O lympic Games
T errific fun
B urnley is the best team
A ce footballer
L ove the game
L eague.

Jack Habiak (5)
Ightenhill Primary School, Burnley

Daddy

D inosaurs are our favourite toys
A nd Daddy is a man who makes me laugh
D inosaurs are real and dangerous
D anger - saving me all the time
Y es, I love you.

Braeden Lee David Robinson (6)
Ightenhill Primary School, Burnley

Football

F an.
O ver the net.
O lympians.
T errific.
B ought a football.
A fast football.
L ies on the pitch.
L ove football.

Charlie Bannister (6)
Ightenhill Primary School, Burnley

Friends

F riendly laughs.
R eally good fun.
I have seven paths.
E veryone is cool.
N ever fall over.
D earest friends.
S miles forever.

Essika Bennett (6)
Ightenhill Primary School, Burnley

Noodles

N ice and stringy
O nly the good ones I like
O nly my favourite
D elicious
L ovely
E ven better than ice cream
S crumptious.

Kian Fitzpatrick (6)
Ightenhill Primary School, Burnley

Dogs

D ogs like biting hard
O lder dogs and younger dogs are clever
G o and meet other dogs to talk
S leep, play, they are very cute and fluffy and like to eat.

Lucy Skaife (6)
Ightenhill Primary School, Burnley

Tigers

T igers are my animals.
I know tigers live in jungles.
G reat animal.
E verybody likes them.
R azor-sharp teeth.
S o cute.

Jake Knight (7)
Ightenhill Primary School, Burnley

Apple

A pples are juicy
P recious they taste
P ink ones are my favourite
L ick my lips, *mmm*
E xcellent fruit.

Emily Bradshaw (6)
Ightenhill Primary School, Burnley

Amaya

A amle is my friend.
M y favourite colour is purple.
A dventurous today.
Y ellow is a colour.
A puppy is cute.

Amaya Trapanese (6)
Ightenhill Primary School, Burnley

Sister

S ister is zero.
I nteresting.
S tar.
T akes turns.
E ggs are nice.
R eally happy.

Daisie Dakota Skyla Humber (6)
Ightenhill Primary School, Burnley

Snake

S nakes are cute
N o snakes aren't cute
A nd precious
K eeping snakes
E nd of snake.

Olivia Steer (6)
Ightenhill Primary School, Burnley

Soup

S oup is my favourite.
O nions are delicious.
U nder the bowl is hot
P eople eat delicious soup.

Star Krasowski (6)
Ightenhill Primary School, Burnley

Gracy

G reat.
R unner.
A dventurous.
C aring.
Y ellow is my favourite.

Gracy Mai Dean (6)
Ightenhill Primary School, Burnley

Red

R ed is my favourite colour
E veryone likes red a lot
D ark red and light red.

Mason Hitchon (6) & Chloe
Ightenhill Primary School, Burnley

Ruby

R ich people.
U ntil my birthday.
B each is fun.
Y ummy food.

Ruby Faragher (7)
Ightenhill Primary School, Burnley

Abu

A bu likes ninjas
B reaktime is when I play football
U sually, we play football

H i, I have a best friend
U nited with school
R ain is pouring down
A lways working hard
I like my family
R onaldo is the best footballer
A lways helpful
H elping my family and friends.

Abu Hurairah (6)
Intack Primary School, Blackburn

Mohammad

M y sister doesn't play with me
O ranges are tasty and yummy
H orrid Henry is my favourite
A lways working hard
M y baby brother is cute
M altesers are the best
A lways helping others
D on't ignore your friends.

Mohammad Ch (6)
Intack Primary School, Blackburn

Fatimah

F atimah is my name
A pples are my favourite fruit
T ea is my favourite
I have two annoying sisters and one annoying brother
M ulticoloured is my favourite
A isha is my favourite cousin
H oola-hooping is my favourite.

Fatimah Zahra S (6)
Intack Primary School, Blackburn

Kornelia

K ornelia is my name
O ctopuses are my favourite animal
R abbits are my favourite animals
N ovember is Bonfire Night
E ggs are yummy
L ions scare me
I like fruit and vegetables
A mna is my friend.

Kornelia Zietek (6)
Intack Primary School, Blackburn

Zack

Z ayn is my friend
A pples are disgusting and watery
C ats are my favourite animals
H arry is on my street
A nts are small
R eading is my favourite thing
Y oghurts are my fourth favourite.

Zack Evans (6)
Intack Primary School, Blackburn

Mariam

M ariam is my first name
A unicorn is my favourite
R abbits are my favourite animal
I ce cream is my favourite
A pples are my favourite fruit
M onkeys are my least favourite animal.

Mariam Malik (6)
Intack Primary School, Blackburn

Jayjay

J ayjay is my name
A ll my friends are nice to me
Y ummy ice cream for my dessert
J ayjay is joyful
A lways reading lots of books
Y es! It's nearly bedtime.

Jayjay Koselka (6)
Intack Primary School, Blackburn

Jessica

J essica likes jelly
E llie-May is my sister
S isters are kind
S inging is fun
I like playing with Play-Doh
C akes are yummy
A lways works hard.

Jessica Archer (6)
Intack Primary School, Blackburn

Arianna

A rianna is my name
R ed is my favourite colour
I am six years old
A nimals are my favourite
N ever tell lies
N ever give up
A lways work hard.

Arianna Patel (6)
Intack Primary School, Blackburn

Michael

M ichael is my name
I like pizza
C hocolate is my favourite
H ot days I love the most
A pples are yummy
E lephants are big
L ollies are yummy.

Michael John D'Alessandro (7)
Intack Primary School, Blackburn

Scarlet

S carlet is my name
C ats are cute
A pples are horrible
R ed is my best colour
L oving are my friends
E ngland is my country
T igers scare me.

Scarlet Maxwell (6)
Intack Primary School, Blackburn

Arissa

A rissa is my name
R achel is my sister
I love red peppers
S aturday is my favourite day
S unday is my favourite day
A rt is my favourite drawing.

Arissa Akhtar (6)
Intack Primary School, Blackburn

Dec

D ec is my name
E very day I play with friends
C hocolate is my favourite
L oves Angry Birds
A ngry Birds sharing my chips
N is for nice Declan.

Declan H (6)
Intack Primary School, Blackburn

Macey

M y favourite cousin is Alexa
A rt is my favourite subject
C ats are my least favourite animal
E mily is my sister
Y ellow is not my favourite colour.

Macey Jade Harrison (7)
Intack Primary School, Blackburn

Lawson

L awson is my name
A pples are my favourite
W heels are my favourite
S hannon is my friend
O ranges are yummy
N ovember is my favourite.

Lawson Yates (6)
Intack Primary School, Blackburn

Salman

S ausages are my favourite
A cting is my hobby
L ove ice lollies
M oora is my friend
A pples are my favourite
N ice friends are kind.

Salman Mahmad (6)
Intack Primary School, Blackburn

Ayesha

A yesha is my name
Y ellow is my favourite colour
E njoy coming to school
S isters are kind
H olidays are fun
A lways try my best.

Ayesha Malic (6)
Intack Primary School, Blackburn

Marva

M ake-up is my favourite
A lways reading lots of books
R elaxing with my cute little sister
V ans are my favourite
A pples are my favourite.

Marva Sheid (7)
Intack Primary School, Blackburn

Malcom

M alcolm is my name
A nd I have a dog and cat
L ily is my friend
C aravans are lovely
O livia is my friend
M y reading is good.

Malcom Davies (6)
Intack Primary School, Blackburn

Marija

M arija is my name
A lways playing basketball
R eading is really fun
I am six years old
J ogging is fun
A lways smiling.

Marija Kiurt (6)
Intack Primary School, Blackburn

Alicia

A licia is my name
L exi is my friend
I ce cream is my good food
C hocolate
I love my mummy
A nimals are my favourite.

Alicia Wright (6)
Intack Primary School, Blackburn

Tillie

T illie likes to play
I love chocolate
L ikes watching TV
L ikes to play with friends
I like my mum
E ggs are yummy.

Tillie S (6)
Intack Primary School, Blackburn

Eduard

E ggs are my favourite food
D ogs are my favourite animals
U nicorns
A re my favourite
R iding up
D ad is my best dad.

Eduard Kevorkyan (6)
Intack Primary School, Blackburn

Eesaa

E esaa is my name
E lephants are my favourite animal
S weets are my favourite
A pples are my favourite
A lligators scare me.

Eesaa Foolat (6)
Intack Primary School, Blackburn

Eshal

E shal likes playing with her friends
S uper friend
H as one brother
A lways trying her best
L oves her friends and family.

Eshal Rhman (6)
Intack Primary School, Blackburn

Alfie

A lfie is my name
L ike chocolate
F ootball is my favourite sport
I like my dog Storm
E lephants are my favourite animal.

Alfie Donnelly (6)
Intack Primary School, Blackburn

Moosa

M oosa likes playing games
O nly play with my friends
O nly work hard
S undays are a day to play games
A lways smiling.

Moosa Nasir (6)
Intack Primary School, Blackburn

Adrian

A drian is my name
D ancing is fun
R unning is good
I like games
A lways work hard
N ever hit people.

Adrian Babiarz (6)
Intack Primary School, Blackburn

Harry

H arry is my name
A pples are nice
R ed is my best colour
R ainy days are boring
Y ellow is the sun's colour.

Harry Andrew Hodgeon (6)
Intack Primary School, Blackburn

Gwen

G wen is my name
W ednesday is my favourite day
E lephants are my favourite animals
N ot the best time to go to sleep.

Gwen Mellor-Best (6)
Intack Primary School, Blackburn

Ella

E ggs are my least favourite food
L unch is my favourite part of the day
L earning is the best
A sthma is the worst.

Ella Maxwel (6)
Intack Primary School, Blackburn

Ahmed

A hmed is my name
H orrid Henry is my show
M onkeys are cheeky
E ggs are yummy
D ecember is my birthday.

Salahuddin Awan Ahmed (6)
Intack Primary School, Blackburn

Wasiq

W asiq is my name
A pples are my favourite
S aturday is fun
I like black
Q ueens live in castles.

Wasiq Nasar (6)
Intack Primary School, Blackburn

Eamon

E amon is my name
A nd I had a cat
M y sister is annoying
O range if my favourite
N ever give up.

Eamon Escels (7)
Intack Primary School, Blackburn

Lawy

L awy likes lollipops
A lways works hard
W ednesday is my best day
Y esterday I watched television.

Lawy Hassan (7)
Intack Primary School, Blackburn

Skye

S kye is my name
K ittens live in my house
Y ou can make me laugh
E ating broccoli is my favourite.

Skye Amber Louise Robinson (7)
Intack Primary School, Blackburn

Lily

L ily is my name
I 'm a princess
L ike to eat chocolate
Y ellow is my favourite colour.

Lily Hargreaves (6)
Intack Primary School, Blackburn

Lexi

L exi is my name
E lephants are my favourite
X ylophone makes music
I love pizza.

Lexi Mc (6)
Intack Primary School, Blackburn

Musa

M usa is my name
U mar is my friend
S weets are my favourite
A pples are the best.

Musa Solkar (6)
Intack Primary School, Blackburn

Leon

L eon is my name
E llie is my pug
O ranges are yummy
N aughty, that isn't me.

Leon Malankowski (6)
Intack Primary School, Blackburn

Orangutan

O rangutans swing at trees
R eady for eating bananas
A sunny day, I'm so excited
N o! Don't chop this tree down
G rass is growing for me to eat
U h-oh, there is a fire in the tree
T rees are cut down for palm oil
A nd my home is being destroyed
N early time for bedtime, I am very tired.

Nina Sadowska (6)
Springfield Community Primary School, Burnley

Orangutan

O rangutan is swinging on the tree
R eady for swinging on the trees
A sunny day and I am so happy
N early time for the tiger's tea
G o and get your tasty food
U nderneath the shade is nice and cool
T he tall trees are my home
A way from the tiger
N ever let that tiger eat me.

Ibrahim Ali (6)
Springfield Community Primary School, Burnley

Orangutan

O rangutans are swinging
R eady to swing to the tree
A nother day for climbing
N ight-time and the rainforest is on fire
G rab the branches to the side
U nderneath the tree, he finds his brother
T he tall tree is where he lives
A lways climbing on the trees
N early time for bed.

Isaac Stanworth
Springfield Community Primary School, Burnley

Orangutan

O rangutan babies are cute
R eady to swing on the tree
A mother orangutan is sleeping
N early time for the baby to swing
G reen grass is great to eat
U nderneath the tree is a tiger
T rees have big green leaves
A nd they are used for me
N early extinct.

Layla-Mae Pounder (6)
Springfield Community Primary School, Burnley

Orangutan

O rangutans are hairy
R un! The tigers will get you
A n orangutan is orange
N early extinct because people are chopping down trees for palm oil
G et in the tree
U h-oh, there's a tiger
T he baby is cute
A tiger it getting me
N o, my mummy!

Holly-Mae Creelman (6)
Springfield Community Primary School, Burnley

Orangutan

O rangutan I told to go away
R ight up towards us
A tiger is coming towards us
N ow the tiger's teeth are sharp
G o, tiger!
U h-oh, there's the tiger
T he sunniest day
A tiger is sleeping near
N ow it's time to sleep.

Ibrahim Tariq (6)
Springfield Community Primary School, Burnley

Orangutan

O rangutans are clever
R un, run up the tree
A tiger is in my forest
N early extinct because homes are destroyed
G ive me some fruit
U nderneath the tree
T rees are my favourite
A hot day
N o tiger, you can't come up here.

Maisie Dean (6)
Springfield Community Primary School, Burnley

Orangutan

O rangutans swing from tree to tree
R un away from the tiger
A tiger has found me!
N ever go to sleep
G o up in the tree
U p in the trees, racing a tiger
T rees are very good
A tiger will get me
N o, don't cut the tree!

Christopher Neil Macdonald (6)
Springfield Community Primary School, Burnley

Orangutan

O range hair
R eady for climbing
A sunny day and I am here
N ow it's time to swing
G et away from me
U nless you stop, I will swing away
T all trees are where I live
A ngry with the tigers
N early time for home.

Aeryn Halson (6)
Springfield Community Primary School, Burnley

Orangutan

O range and beautiful
R oll and live
A nd cannot survive in the jungle
N o! You can't destroy my home
G o from my home!
U nder hot shade
T all and strong
A sunny day, I'm happy
N ow I'm going to sleep.

Irfa Amir (6)
Springfield Community Primary School, Burnley

Orangutan

O rangutans are
R eady for swinging
A lways swinging in the trees
N ever touch the ground
G etting ready for the season
U nderneath the trees
T hey're digging
A lways swinging
N early finished.

Olivia-Rose Debra Ellis (6)
Springfield Community Primary School, Burnley

Orangutan

O rangutans are smart
R oaring tiger
A tiger, run!
N o, don't cut the tree down
G rooming in the tree
U nder the warm tree
T igers can't get me
A tiger, argh!
N o, you can't get me!

Noah Franklin (6)
Springfield Community Primary School, Burnley

Orangutan

O range animals
R un far away
A nd swing fast
N ice in the trees
G iant trees I'm in
U nderground worms
T rees are cut down
A nd tigers are going to get me
N ow it's time to sleep.

Thomas Callum Fuller (6)
Springfield Community Primary School, Burnley

Orangutan

O rangutans are funny
R eally funny
A nd not scary
N ot to go into the water
G o up in the green trees
U p high they swing
T hey go on land
A nd look for food
N ever touch me.

Amy Walker (6)
Springfield Community Primary School, Burnley

Orangutan

O range hair
R eally hairy
A nd swinging around
N ot green
G o into the green trees
U p high they swing
T hey're big
A nd clever
N ot stupid.

Coby Ewens (6)
Springfield Community Primary School, Burnley

Local Area

L ocal areas are ordinary areas
O ur area has to be looked after
C ome to eat in the cafe shop
A fter you have gone somewhere
L ook after it, you have to tidy

A fter you've made a mess, clean up
R ed post box
E verywhere you go and you see a mess, tidy up
A lways take care of your local area.

Saalih Kamran (6)
St Luke & St Philip's CE Primary School, Blackburn

Local Area

L ook at our beautiful area
O ff we go to the chip shop
C an you see a bus stop
A nd a school?
L ook up to the sky

A ll the shops are busy, look out for the red post box, always look after your area
R ide a bike on the street
E at chips in the chip shop
A lways make your area tidy.

Mohammad Ismail (6)
St Luke & St Philip's CE Primary School, Blackburn

Local Area

L ook at our beautiful area
O ur local area is so nice
C an we see a physical feature?
A ll our houses are tinted
L ook, can you see a human feature?

A ll local areas are the best
R ocks int he beautiful playground
E njoy sweets from the shop
A ll local areas are wonderful.

Mark Madden (6)
St Luke & St Philip's CE Primary School, Blackburn

Local Area

L ook around
O ff we go to the chippy
C an you see the wonderful orange flowers
A ll the wonderful flowers
L ots of wonderful things

A lot of houses on the street
R ed post boxes
E ating soups and lots of noises
A t bedtime, all the lamp posts are turned on.

Ella Dean (6)
St Luke & St Philip's CE Primary School, Blackburn

Local Area

L ovely local area
O h, look at the pretty flowers
C ome to the playground
A t our school
L ook around

A t our local area, there is a chip shop
R emember to give instructions
E very day we're at school
A t the playground, there are fun things.

Alicja Karwowska (6)
St Luke & St Philip's CE Primary School, Blackburn

Local Area

L ook all around the school
O ur coffee shop
C an you see the beautiful trees
A nd physical features
L ook at our local area

A nd look at the chip shop
R ed flowers on the beautiful grass
E nd of the walk
A lways take care of your local area.

Rahaan Craigh (6)
St Luke & St Philip's CE Primary School, Blackburn

Local Area

L ook around
O ur local area
C an you take a picture?
A nd look at our beautiful flowers
L ook at our school

A nd remember to come again
R emember to come every day
E verybody enjoys fish and chips
A nd come to the playground to play.

Amanda-Jayne Bleeks (6)
St Luke & St Philip's CE Primary School, Blackburn

Local Area

L ook at the local area
O r look at the orange flowers
C an you see a beautiful school?
A nd look at the houses
L ook at the beautiful trees.

A nd look at the clouds
R ed post boxes
E ating tiny sausages
A t the chip shop.

Hope McCleary (6)
St Luke & St Philip's CE Primary School, Blackburn

Local Area

L ook after our local area
O range flowers
C offee shop
A nd a chip shop
L ovely lunch in the chip shop

A nd eating sandwiches at the coffee shop
R ed, beautiful flowers growing
E ating chips and sandwiches
A mazing area.

Lexi Freya Mcalinden (6)
St Luke & St Philip's CE Primary School, Blackburn

Local Area

L ook at my street
O ff we go to the shop
C an you see a playground?
A ll the people are playing.
L ook around at the trees

A nd look at the houses
R ead a book
E xciting aeroplanes in the sky
A nyone can do anything.

Samme Abdullah (6)
St Luke & St Philip's CE Primary School, Blackburn

Local Area

L ook around the place
O h, it's so beautiful
C an you see the sun
A nd the clouds in the sky
L ook at the plants

A nd the green trees
R ound the school, we can play
E njoy the playground
A lways tidy your area.

Daniel Obiefna (6)
St Luke & St Philip's CE Primary School, Blackburn

Local Area

L ovely flowers
O utside the chip shop
C an you smell the chips?
A nd a coffee shop.
L ocal area.

A nd look at the chips
R ed flower
E ating from the chip shop
A mazing local area is amazing.

Daniyal Tanveer (6)
St Luke & St Philip's CE Primary School, Blackburn

Local Area

L ook at our school
O range flowers are growing
C an you see a bus stop
A nd a chip shop?
L ook at the houses

A nd the cars
R ocks in the garden
E ating chips
A eroplanes in the sky.

Mikolaj Sobiecki
St Luke & St Philip's CE Primary School, Blackburn

Local Area

L ovely flowers
O range flowers growing
C ars driving
A nd a red post box
L ovely lunch

A nd a nice coffee shop
R ed flowers
E ating chips
A lways take care of your area.

Jordan Morrison (6)
St Luke & St Philip's CE Primary School, Blackburn

Local Area

L ook around
O range flowers
C an you see a house?
A car is special
L ovely park

A pples on the trees
R ainbow in the sky
E ating chippy
A pples shaking in the trees.

Bradley Greenwood (6)
St Luke & St Philip's CE Primary School, Blackburn

Local Area

L ovely flowers
O range flowers
C offee shop
A coffee shop
L ook at our local area

A beautiful sun
R ed flowers sitting there
E ating chips
A mazing local area.

Rhiana Mercer (6)
St Luke & St Philip's CE Primary School, Blackburn

Local Area

L ovely flowers
O range flowers
C offee shop
A wesome cars
L ook at the flowers

A nd the red post box
R ed cars
E ating fish and chips
A nd eating sandwiches.

Awab Haroon (6)
St Luke & St Philip's CE Primary School, Blackburn

Local Area

L ocal road
O range
C ars
A pples
L ook

A t
R obots
E ggs
A rea.

Raul Cosmin (6)
St Luke & St Philip's CE Primary School, Blackburn

Florence

F lorence is lovely and kind.
L ovely people like me.
O h, lovely people help people who are ill.
R eally good people love learning.
E arly people like me, get up and play.
N ever lasting, people like me love learning.
C aring people love others.
E xcellent, loving people always help.

Florence Rowen (6)
St Patrick's RC Primary School, Walton-le-Dale

Eva

M y lovely mummy has so many hugs.
A really good dancer.
C lever as can be.
K ind to all my friends.
E veryone likes me.
N ice to everyone.
Z ebras are cool and I like them.
I love to go to the park.
E va is amazing.

Eva Mackenzie (6)
St Patrick's RC Primary School, Walton-le-Dale

Caitlin

C aring Caitlin is my name.
A lways smiling with a happy face.
I s always doing kind things.
T ells her friends compliments.
L oves her family very much
I s always being lovely.
N ever ever gives up.

Caitlin Parker (6)
St Patrick's RC Primary School, Walton-le-Dale

Scarlet

S ings in a beautiful voice.
C ats are my favourite.
A lways a lovely helper.
R abbits are my favourite.
L ollies are my favourite sweet.
E verything is wonderful.
T akes turns with my friends.

Scarlet-Rose Mayne (6)
St Patrick's RC Primary School, Walton-le-Dale

Brodie

B rodie is a role model.
R unning in football is fun.
O ne day I will be a striker.
D elightful for this world.
I am happy when I go to school.
E very day I love my friends.

Brodie Pilkington (7)
St Patrick's RC Primary School, Walton-le-Dale

Amelia

A mazing, just wonderful girl.
M akes sure to look after her friends.
E xcellent, helpful friend.
L ovely, helpful friend.
I nteresting and wonderful.
A good dancer.

Amelia Jewes-Bonage (6)
St Patrick's RC Primary School, Walton-le-Dale

Brooke

B usy, pretty, kind.
R eally funny, super funny!
O nce she started dancing.
O nly just pierced her ears.
K ept her Easter garden.
E very day she enjoys school.

Brooke Amelia Furesz (6)
St Patrick's RC Primary School, Walton-le-Dale

Oliver

O liver is an amazing friend.
L oves playing Minecraft.
I s very caring.
V ery creative.
E very day he likes to play.
R eally loves his family.

Oliver James Johnstone (6)
St Patrick's RC Primary School, Walton-le-Dale

Seamus

S eamus is a good writer.
E xciting maths.
A good friend.
M um is a teacher.
U nbelievable swimmer.
S eamus is a good Jiu Jitsu-er.

Seamus Alty (6)
St Patrick's RC Primary School, Walton-le-Dale

Kaleb

K iwi is my favourite food.
A pples are yummy.
L ovely mummy is mine.
E lephants are my favourite animal.
B arbecue is my favourite food.

Kaleb Colapinto (6)
St Patrick's RC Primary School, Walton-le-Dale

Hollie

H appy when I am playing.
O n green, always.
L oves school.
L oving to friends.
I ce cream is my favourite.
E njoying school.

Hollie Calvert (6)
St Patrick's RC Primary School, Walton-le-Dale

Alfie

A mazing Alfie is the best.
L ovely boy and lovely friend.
F antastic person that loves otters.
I 'm mature
E veryone's friend.

Alfie Parkinson (7)
St Patrick's RC Primary School, Walton-le-Dale

Jacob

J oins in with lots of games.
A lways helps people.
C an play football.
O ne day I will be a policeman.
B oxing is my favourite game.

Jacob Walmsley (6)
St Patrick's RC Primary School, Walton-le-Dale

Connor

C onnor is happy.
O ne good, brilliant person.
N av is nice to me.
N ever bad in school.
O ne good person.
R eady to run.

Connor Boyle (6)
St Patrick's RC Primary School, Walton-le-Dale

Maisie

M aisie is beautiful.
A lways smiling.
I 'm a superstar.
S ix years old.
I love my family.
E veryone's friend.

Maisie Wright (6)
St Patrick's RC Primary School, Walton-le-Dale

Emily

E mily is wonderful.
M y friends are important.
I am always kind to my friends.
L ove my family.
Y ellow is my favourite colour.

Emily Gudgeon (6)
St Patrick's RC Primary School, Walton-le-Dale

Laura

L ikes swimming.
A ways kind to her friends.
U nderstands the school rules.
R eally good at writing.
A lways plays with her toys.

Jessica Leighton (6)
St Patrick's RC Primary School, Walton-le-Dale

Archie

A rchie.
R ed is good.
C at games are good.
H is games are good.
I like you.
E verything is good.

Archie Joseph Lord (6)
St Patrick's RC Primary School, Walton-le-Dale

Alfie

A lfie likes eating apples.
L oves Roblox.
F riends are special.
I like Roblox.
E verybody likes me.

Alfie Sean Hodson (6)
St Patrick's RC Primary School, Walton-le-Dale

Evan

E ats chocolate all the time.
V ery good at Minecraft.
A lways trying to be good.
N ever unkind.

Evan Beau Turner (7)
St Patrick's RC Primary School, Walton-le-Dale

Erin

E rin is lovely and kind.
R eally good swimmer.
I 'm good at games.
N ice writer.

Erin Boyle (6)
St Patrick's RC Primary School, Walton-le-Dale

Tarantula

T errifying people so they go away and no one can harm it.
A scary creature creeping in people's houses.
R eally hideous because it's frightening everyone because the people are annoying.
A hairy spider crawling on people's hands.
N aughty spider going onto people's backs to tickle them.
T arantula eats bees, slugs, worms and insects.
U nreal at killing worms softly.
L ikes playing with other adult spiders all the time.
A hairy spider that most likes to kill things.

Muhammad Mogra (6)
St Paul's CE Primary School, Astley Bridge

Ice Castle

I cy, mystical palace in the forest
C amouflage with a lot of snow
E cho-maker that is so loud you can hear it at the zoo

C ool kangaroo as a pet dancing on the street
A pricot-lover inside my heart
S ee-through building because of the snow
T he snow has made me white
L ovely leaves dancing across my head
E pic building in the distance.

Laila Khan (6)
St Paul's CE Primary School, Astley Bridge

Lion

L azy, lying lion sleeping in a jungle.
I love eating meat.
O mnivores are disgusting.
N aughty animals attack me.

J umping, strong animal.
A black animal.
G etting annoying makes me angry.
U gly animals make me chuckle.
A nimals think I'm the strongest.
R unning fast is what it does.

Sobaan Raza (6)
St Paul's CE Primary School, Astley Bridge

November

N ice boy on every exciting birthday
O n Monday, it's my big birthday
V ery big parties make me crazy
E veryone comes to my party
M y birthday is very special because I'm born on it
B ig parties make me the happiest
E veryone looks different and I don't know who is who
R un very fast and watch balloons.

Zaid R'Honi (6)
St Paul's CE Primary School, Astley Bridge

Abdoulie

A good footballer that always scores goals.
B oring person who loves watching television.
D ancer that is super energetic.
O utstanding person who thinks of others.
U nderstanding maths like a genius.
L onely person sometimes.
I 'm not a vegetarian person.
E pic person who makes weird poses.

Abdoulie Bah (6)
St Paul's CE Primary School, Astley Bridge

Unicorn

U nicorns delight me with wonder and make me smile.
N ice songs come from the unicorn's mouth.
I n the sky, the unicorns glide beautifully.
C otton candy eater.
O n the moon, the unicorn makes a lovely shadow.
R ainbows are the unicorns' favourite thing.
N ice smile makes people fall in love.

Zainab Mitha (7)
St Paul's CE Primary School, Astley Bridge

Muhammad

M y name is Muhammad.
U sing magic, I can run faster than a cheetah.
H andles are better than fingers.
A boy is a master.
M y mum is the best because she loves me.
M y friend is Zaid and we play tig.
A nd I am clever when I do lots of tables.
D ad is funny because he loses his car keys.

Muhammad Yasin (6)
St Paul's CE Primary School, Astley Bridge

Rainbow

R ainbows are so colourful
A nice flower could smell nice
I n a hot, sunny day, I could eat ice cream
N ice books are my favourite to read
B ows are my favourite
O n a snowy day, I love to build a snowman
W inning a cup in sports is what I wanted
S wimming is my favourite challenge.

Reyhand Ali (6)
St Paul's CE Primary School, Astley Bridge

Dinosaur

D aring, dangerous, deadly dinosaur
I rritating and powerful giant
N aughty, nosy, nuisance
O verprotective and outstanding
S trong, evil stomper
A huge dinosaur who is a herbivore
U nhappy when I don't eat delicious food
R oaring is what I don't do!

Zakariya Maka (7)
St Paul's CE Primary School, Astley Bridge

Kitten

K ittens do not like cold water.
I n the front room, the kitten is mischevious.
T he kitten loves to scratch the sofa.
T he kitten loves to be lazing on her toys.
E ating cat food because that is her favourite treat.
N ow at night-time, she wakes up and rolls on the carpet.

Maryam Buksh (6)
St Paul's CE Primary School, Astley Bridge

Family

F antastic family that I've seen
A n amazing sister that hugs me a lot
M um makes me mouth-watering food
I like my little sister very much and she talks a lot
L ovely family that keeps me safe
Y ou are a beautiful family and you are so sweet.

Buella Koteh (7)
St Paul's CE Primary School, Astley Bridge

Kitten

K itten is lazy and crazy
I like rainbows that are glittery
T ends to play a lot and it's super fun
T ins to chew that are rainbow
E ating so much that it makes my tummy full
N ight howler that's so loud, it awakes everyone in the house.

Hayaa Zaidi (6)
St Paul's CE Primary School, Astley Bridge

Matilda

M atilda is a very clever girl.
A really good cook and reader.
T ogether people make friends with Matilda.
I ncredible and clever.
L ovely little child that believes in herself.
D ecorates anything.
A mazing magician and a dancer.

Aaminah Patel (6)
St Paul's CE Primary School, Astley Bridge

Beach

B eautiful sunshine reflects on the water.
E ating chips at the beach but cheeky seagulls eat the chips!
A mazing surfing and I'm a good swimmer.
C elebrating in the water and splashing.
H appy children splashing or making sandcastles.

Mariam Doodhwala (6)
St Paul's CE Primary School, Astley Bridge

Pirates

P irates like to travel across tropical seas
I ncredibly brave
R ed Beard is a fierce pirate
A dventurous people
T errifying everyone on the deck
E ver so smelly
S o dumb because they didn't go to school.

Hidayah Chhadat (6)
St Paul's CE Primary School, Astley Bridge

Unicorn

U p high in the sky.
N ice creature and great flyer.
I n the sky, flying happily.
C andy eater.
O n the soft cloud, they like to jump.
R eally nice.
N ever naughty.
S tylish mammal prancing along.

Chidinma Nwandiogo (6)
St Paul's CE Primary School, Astley Bridge

Kittens

K ittens are better because dogs alway chase me
I love my friends because they always play with me
T he dogs are always mean to me
T iny and fluffy
E ating food
N ibbling cat food all day.

Katie-Lee Dawson (6)
St Paul's CE Primary School, Astley Bridge

Rahman

R E is easy because I concentrating
A nd our class are super writers
H e is a brilliant worker
M y favourite thing is chocolate cake
A nd people are good workers
N obody has been silly.

Rahman Ahmed (6)
St Paul's CE Primary School, Astley Bridge

Faria

F unny poses in pictures
A lways excited to go on holiday
R eally cheeky at home by putting my dolls in Safa's face
I love going to gymnastics and doing flips
A lways being a weirdo at home.

Faria Dakri (6)
St Paul's CE Primary School, Astley Bridge

Spider

S ome spiders are scary
P eople are terrified of spiders
I don't like spiders
D angling from its web
E ats flies and insects
R ain makes them curl into a big ball.

Abdullahi Muhidin Ali (6)
St Paul's CE Primary School, Astley Bridge

Panther

P owerful and strange and fantastic
A super jumper
N ow everyone is scared
T errified of puma
H unter of puma
E very day it's hard
R ipping the skin.

Faraj Sasi (6)
St Paul's CE Primary School, Astley Bridge

Faraz

F ast and catching my friends.
A fter school, I watch cartoons.
R ahman is my friend.
A lways my brother makes me sad.
Z ooming around the playground at playtime.

Faraz Ahmad (7)
St Paul's CE Primary School, Astley Bridge

Panther

P owerful scratch.
A strong bite.
N ight hunter.
T ricks animals.
H e is strong.
E ats a lot of food.
R eaches from tree to tree.

Aaryan Nazir (6)
St Paul's CE Primary School, Astley Bridge

Rainbow

R ainbows are beautiful
A ll different colours
I am bright
N ever close to the sun
B e kind
O ver the houses
W et rain on me.

Aymen (7)
St Paul's CE Primary School, Astley Bridge

Horse

H appy horse eating hay
O mnivores are disgusting
R acer that always wins
S illy horse making noise
E very day I chase my friends on the farm.

Neema Hekeleme (6)
St Paul's CE Primary School, Astley Bridge

Bella

B ella is faster when she is playing.
E xcited to go to the park.
L ovely hair.
L aughs every day.
A lways wonderful and cute.

Bella Farrell (6)
St Paul's CE Primary School, Astley Bridge

Maha

M y favourite thing to do is running fast.
A ways eating pizza.
H igh jumping in the sky.
A lways playing football fast.

Maha Aslam (6)
St Paul's CE Primary School, Astley Bridge

Jack

J elly is my favourite food.
A really fast runner.
C lever.
K ind boy.

Jack Buckthorpe
St Paul's CE Primary School, Astley Bridge

Dubai

D ancers are very good at dancing
U nder the sky is blue
B allerinas are very amazing
A t ballet
I t's the best!

Husna Bux (7)
St Pius X Catholic Preparatory School, Fulwood

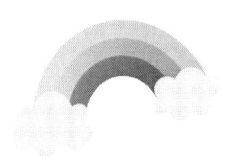

Lions

L iving lions
I see roaring lions
O n top of a mountain
N ot sleepy but creepy
S leepy now near me in my dream.

Zaid Khan (7)
St Pius X Catholic Preparatory School, Fulwood

Young Writers Information

We hope you have enjoyed reading this book – and that you will continue to in the coming years.

If you're a young writer who enjoys reading and creative writing, or the parent of an enthusiastic poet or story writer, do visit our website **www.youngwriters.co.uk**. Here you will find free competitions, workshops and games, as well as recommended reads, a poetry glossary and our blog. There's lots to keep budding writers motivated to write!

If you would like to order further copies of this book, or any of our other titles, then please give us a call or order via your online account.

Young Writers
Remus House
Coltsfoot Drive
Peterborough
PE2 9BF
(01733) 890066
info@youngwriters.co.uk

Join in the conversation!
Tips, news, giveaways and much more!

YoungWritersUK   @YoungWritersCW